Endorsements

J oe Shelley is a man of God! I have known Joe for more
than twenty years. He has been through many trials
and tribulations, but with the help of the Lord, his faith
has never faltered. It has grown deeper. Life's experiences have taught Joe many things, but most of all, he has
learned to trust in God and walk closely with Him.

This book is well worth reading and keeping near at
hand. There is so much evil in the world that fathers need
to be wise and walk closely with the Lord to survive and
give guidance to their children. Joe has shown us the way

to do this. "A Father's Approval" is written from the heart! God will bless you as you read it.

Dr. Robert W. Otto

(WWII Prisoner of War, Author, Friend of Joe)

So much of what I teach and share in my books and seminars is to help people discover their greatness. Joe has written a book that explores the impact, both positive and negative, a father makes in the life of his children. His insight into this subject of a father's approval will provoke you at the core of your being. This book provides you vital tools to find healing in your relationship with your father and your children. Once you read "A Father's Approval", you will see things differently and make choices that positively influence your role as father.

Brian Klemmer, author of the best seller

"Compassionate Samurai"

A number of years ago, a friend of mine found an advertisement for workers needed to work on the Al-Can highway. It was hidden by brush and debris. When he cleared it away, he found that the sign said, "Wanted Men – We Mean Men – None else need apply!" The sign was intended to lure men who could face the harsh winter conditions of the Canadian and Alaskan Tundra. I have found Joe Shelley to be such a man! Not with the weather conditions of the tundra; but with the harsh realities of life. I have found him to be a "Man of Godly Character" and who is unashamed to pour his life into others who need help. He especially has a heart for children. His life has modeled the chapters of this book.

Although it has been many years since my husband and I had the privilege to serve as pastors to Joe, Sue, Amy, Hannah, and Joy, we became close friends to them, and we have kept in touch through these many years. Joe and Sue did not stop influencing children when their natural children became adults. They have adopted and are pouring themselves into more children who needed parents.

The focus of this book is founded upon the principle that fathers are the most important commodity in shaping the lives of children. The material included in this book is time immemorial truths that Joe has walked out in his life. They have proven to be the foundations upon which lives can and will be changed in families around the world.

Sherry Thompson, Women's Ministries Director,
West Florida District of the Assemblies of God

My wife and I have had the pleasure of knowing Joe Shelley and his family for over eight years. As his Pastor, since he moved to Spokane, Washington, I've been able to not only watch him as a husband and father to his own family, but have witnessed him being a father to many other people, young and not so young.

Joe shares valuable insight in his book "A Father's Approval" from his own life story of pain, hurt and loss. Instead of getting bitter, Joe got better. As you follow along with Joe through the book on his journey in seeking his father's approval, it will grip your heart and soul.

The chapters that Joe talks about 'Unintentional Hurts' and 'Dealing with Offenses' are not only experiences that Joe had to deal with, but he gives the reader several practical steps and insight to bring freedom to the reader as well.

I would recommend "A Father's Approval" to not only every father, but to mothers as well, to assist them in parenting your children or grandchildren. This book will give you Bible-based instruction written from a man who has dared to be vulnerable and transparent so individuals can learn from his journey.

John MacPherson, Senior Pastor Zion Christian Center, Spokane, Washington

A Father's Approval

Leaving a Legacy

Joseph Shelley

Table of Contents

This book is dedicated to my father.

I love you, Dad, and truly thank you for all that you have taught me about life.

Acknowledgements

—ɯɯ—

First and foremost, I must honor and thank my Lord and Savior Jesus Christ, without His love and direction there would be no reason to write this book.

To my wife Sue, who walks in grace, my best friend, lover, and mother to our children I am extremely grateful. When I fell in love with and married you, I made a commitment to love and cherish you for a lifetime. You have made this adventure easy for me and have taught me so much. Without you, I would not know the extreme joy of being a father to our five daughters. My love for you is unconditional and for eternity.

To my beloved Amy, you are awesome and make me very proud to be your dad. When you were born, there was no happier father anywhere in the universe. I still feel that way today. I appreciate your grace as first-born in allowing me to learn to be a daddy. You are full of life and have a boundless love for our Heavenly Father. I appreciate the love and friendship we share together. I love you beyond words.

To my Hannah, the grace of God, where did the time go? I was just in Belgium yesterday holding my new four-thousand three-hundred and seven gram (nine pounds and eight ounces) daughter in my arms. You were my little shadow growing up and you always had to sit next to me. You introduced me to the wonderful privilege of being a grandpa. You will always have a special place in my heart and I love you so much.

To my Joyful one, I still remember the day I became your daddy. I promised myself that I would love you and take care of you the rest of the life we share together. You have lived up to your name and have been a wonderful daughter. When you came to us, Amy and Hannah were at an age of doing their own things, but you stuck by my side and became my little buddy. Now that you are a teenager, you still make me feel so important in your life. I so appreciate how you have embraced your relationship with our Heavenly Daddy. I will love you forever Joy.

To my victorious one, Nicole, who has overcome and blossomed so. You were such a frightened little girl when we rescued you. It broke my heart and I wanted to protect you from all the pain you were going through. I knew what you needed was a daddy who would love you, protect you, and tell you how proud he was of you. The day the adoption was final was such a day of celebration, I was officially your daddy and it was one of the greatest days of my life. I will forever love being your daddy.

To my gift from God, Jasmine, you have filled this daddy heart with so much love. You do not have the words "give up" in your vocabulary and this has been important as you have had to overcome so much. One of your greatest gifts is your ability to serve others which has blessed so many people. I will love you forever.

To Nathaniel, my grandson, your little hands have a big grip on my heart. I absolutely love being your grandpa and being a hero and mentor in your life. My hope is the imprint I make on your life will allow you to become one of the best fathers and daddies this world has ever seen. Your influence will be felt for many generations that will follow you. I love you, buddy.

Introduction

—꘠—

The seed for this book germinated in 1995 when I heard my father tell me, for the first time, "Son, I'm proud of you." The impact of these words began a life-changing journey. This journey took me to new levels of understanding the father heart, as well as healing in areas of my life I didn't even know I needed it. Some of the events of the journey were wonderful, and some were very painful.

I began this book several years ago, but it was nothing more than a few pages worth of notes. It did not amount to much on paper; however, I found myself continually interacting with people on this topic. I have counseled many people on the subjects in this book and have seen numerous relationships healed. Several people have told me that I needed to write a book on the subject. I always justified not writing it because I had convinced myself that I was not a writer and I did not feel qualified to write a book. My excuses were just that - excuses.

The owner of the company I work for asked his leaders to go through the book, "Eating the Elephant One Bite at a Time", by Brian Klemmer. I have to be honest and tell you that I was a little resistant at first, but, in going through the lessons, found the book to be interesting and very challenging. At the end of one of the lessons, the author asked us to write down the biggest difference we felt we had made in our lifetime. Then he suggested we envision how that difference had impacted all of the people touched by this difference we felt we had made. He wanted us to realize we had indeed impacted thousands of lives. Then he asked us to write a page in our journal on how we might make twice that difference, or, even more. The first thing that came to mind was writing this book. I realized that it had the potential to affect millions of people's lives. Sadly, I did nothing more than the journaling assignment.

Then our owner wanted us to go with him to the Personal Mastery Course held by Klemmer and Associates. I agreed to go, but, to be truthful, my motivation had more to do with the fact that I had never been to Whitefish or Kalispell, Montana, and have always wanted to visit there, not to mention it would be a great time of fellowship with my friends! Be that as it may, God had something else in mind.

One of the assignments was to come up with a ninety day goal and have someone hold you accountable to that. At first, I could not think of any goals and then the idea for this book hit me when someone said that if you commit to writing for thirty minutes a day, for ninety days, you could write a book. The bottom line is that I committed to having a rough draft of this book to a publisher in ninety days, which would be July 19, 2009. When I got home, the floodgates opened and I could not stop writing. Here I am not even sixty days from when I started and the bulk of this book is accomplished.

What made me think that I was qualified to write this book? Well, I did spend twenty-five years in the United States Air Force and I reached the highest enlisted rank of Chief Master Sergeant. During those years, I was also a First Sergeant and was responsible for the morale and discipline of the troops. The First Sergeant is the daddy of the unit, the one who takes care of the troops, and the one the troops run to when they're in trouble. I had many awards, decorations, and plaques for my accomplishments. It was a great career. These things might look good on a resume and they did teach me many things about discipline, serving, and managing people, but they are not the main reasons I write this book. The real things that qualify me to write this book are the events in my life as a husband of over twenty-eight years, a son for forty-eight years, and a father of five children and at this time one grandchild. Add those together I guess you would say I have a hundred and nine years of experience. If that is not enough you must understand that I feel strongly that God has taught me so much about a father's approval and a father's impact that He wanted me to write this book. Through the years, I have ministered to hundreds of people in the military, lead men's ministries, and lead fellowship groups, as well as preached in church services about this very subject.

The last fourteen years have been exciting, frustrating, exhausting, enlightening, rewarding, and above all, healing. If it were not for the support of my Lord, my wife, my children, my heroes, and my mentors, this book would not have been written. Some of these chapters might bring you to tears. Some of the chapters might make you upset. Most of these chapters should make you think. My greatest hope is that you will find healing and wholeness so that you will be able to pass love and approval on to the ones you cherish and the generations to follow you.

My Story

—∭—

December 1994, when I was 33 years old, was the first time I heard my father say, "Son, I'm proud of you." Little did I know this would begin a healing process. God knew what He was doing. Those words broke something in me. I no longer felt the need to prove myself to anyone.

At 3:15 AM on a Saturday morning in early February 1995, I received a shocking phone call from the Sheriff's department. One of my friends had just committed suicide leaving behind a wife and two young children. At church, the next day, my Pastor held me in his arms and we cried together. He said to me "Joe, I believe you are asking God why you are in the middle of this, and I believe God is saying that He wants to teach you the Father's heart." This was going to influence my life more than I knew.

He was a man who had committed his life to the Lord at a young age. He and his wife were school sweethearts. They were heavily involved in their youth group. After they married, they were active in their church. They had two beautiful daughters. They had a lovely home, nice cars, and everything looked good. Then it came crashing down on him. He lost his job and could not find another one. His finances fell apart. He was overwhelmed, in depression and began isolating himself. He was a good man! Unfortunately, he believed a lie from the pit of hell, and took his own life. One part of his note said that this was the only way that he knew how to take care of his family financially. The life insurance policy paid even if the cause of death was suicide. He believed he was taking care of his family and that they would be better off without him. The truth is- he was the security of his family, as well as his daughters' hero. His family needed him and loved him no matter what he was going through. He didn't grasp hold of this. What he didn't realize was that his act would shatter the lives of those he left behind.

God taught me the first of many lessons about understanding the Father's heart through this tragedy. First, a daddy's true heart never intends to hurt the ones he loves, though sometimes he does. Secondly, a dad is supposed to be a hero, friend, and mentor. Thirdly, a dad is security for his family. My friend hurt his family. They lost their hero, and the security of the family was shattered. Is this what he had intended? Absolutely not!

In May 1995, one of my closest friend's three-year-old son fell from a balcony three stories high at an apartment complex. He landed on the cement sidewalk below. On their way to the hospital, my friend called me, even before his extended family – wow, who am I? I rushed to the hospital just in time to see the boy's little body being put into the helicopter. They quickly flew him to the trauma center. I spent the next seventy-two hours in the Intensive Care Unit and numerous hours over the next several months in two different hospitals with the family. I'm not special, but I felt the pain my friends were going through.

At one point, my friends needed a break, so I sat alone in the room with their son, looking at his swollen body with all kinds of tubes attached everywhere. The doctors told us that the pressure in his brain was going to kill him unless it started to come down. They gave no hope. I was crying and pleading with God, asking why. At that moment, with a child-like faith, I asked God to show me that this little boy was going to be okay. I asked God an impossible task – to lower the brain pressure. In a split second, the monitor started to beep and then began to drop one point at a time until it was at a normal level. Praise God! – Thank you – the boy was going to be okay. Although we moved away several months later, I did see them a couple of years later at my brother's memorial service, and this little boy was a healthy, normal child.

What was God teaching me through this? A father needs to have the faith of a little child. The story doesn't end there and is a very humbling experience for me. In December 1995, my friend shared at church about what Christmas meant to him and his family. He said that he had an understanding of what the Heavenly Father went through when He lost His Son. He then talked about the impact a father makes on his family and how important his family had become to him. He ended his talk by saying that he wasn't able to see his real father much, but it was okay, because he had a mentor and father there and his name was Joe Shelley. I was amazed! What an impact. God taught me that a father must be available, especially during the hard times.

Throughout the years, several more things happened that affected my life. I underwent the first of eight knee surgeries. My own father had two heart attacks and surgery. My father-in-law underwent quadruple bi-pass heart surgery. One of my wife's aunts was diagnosed with ovarian cancer. One of my brothers'-in-law fell from a barn roof and almost lost his life. He ended up in the same intensive care unit as the boy mentioned earlier with the same type of injuries—he never recovered fully, but he did commit his life to the Lord in February 1996. These were all hard times, each with its own set of questions and lessons about a father's impact.

I had learned so much about a Father's heart, but God wasn't finished with me yet. On December 22, 1995, God woke me up and helped me dictate a letter to my Dad. I will share a few portions of the letter in a later chapter called "Dealing with Offenses."

1997 was to be one of the hardest years of my life. I must reiterate that God is a gracious and loving Father who knows what He is doing. On April 17, I received a phone call informing me that my younger brother, Tim, had just drowned while fishing in Colorado. This could not be happening. I was in shock. We had to arrange to fly from the little town in Florida where we were stationed, to our home in Washington State. My pastor comforted me and, between him and the church family, we got home.

The funeral and memorial service were painful, but nothing compared to when I had to view his body in the casket. The door to the room seemed unmovable, but I pressed on. The emotion was excruciating, but God's peace eventually overwhelmed me. My brother had struggled long trying to find himself, and approval for who he was. I was always concerned about Tim, and about his relationship with God. However, just three months before his death, Tim called me and told me that he had rededicated his life to God and he was doing great. Several more phone calls followed before his death – one just a few days before. During each phone call, Tim stated that he was reading his Bible, going to church, and doing great with God. In the viewing room, I felt God tell me that I didn't have to worry about Tim anymore; he was at home with the Father.

Another person that caused me concern was my father. Dad and I held each other many times and cried, but he was mad at God for taking his son. He told me that he yelled at God and asked why God didn't take him instead of Tim. I looked Dad in the eyes and told him that he wasn't ready to meet His maker, Tim was. Dad conceded this and then said to me, with great pain, "Now I know what God had to go through when His Son died." Dad's life changed dramatically and he began to serve God again.

1997 was also one of the happiest years we have had. We adopted a beautiful little 15-month-old bundle of joy. She is an amazingly awesome young woman. She has brought boundless love and much joy into our family.

I only tell you the next part of this story, as hopefully, it will help someone dealing with the loss of a loved one. I hope it will help some to see how it can happen for a good man or woman to destroy not only their life, but impact generations; and to help them not to make judgments that will haunt them. I believe my Dad would want me to tell this story to help someone recover who might be in similar circumstances.

After a few years, Dad began a downward spiral, falling away from God and the ones who loved him. He started hanging out with friends who were using him and his money. Once again, bitterness took hold of Dad's heart. In 2001, my Dad started disappearing for five to seven days at a time, leaving my Mom all alone and terribly worried about him. Several times, my Mom was so worried that she called the police to file a missing persons report. My Dad was so angry and bitter at everything. His dreams seemed to be shattered and he was losing his footing on reality and life. In November 2001, Dad came home after being gone for several days and told my Mom that he didn't love her anymore. He wanted to live the rest of the life he had left, to do the things he wanted to do. He left after forty-nine years of marriage. My Mom wasn't doing well physically and the siblings moved her to an assisted living home. Mom's strong relationship with God and love for her family has carried her for many years. Dad never left the area. He was hanging out with his buddies. The power of association is so strong; people either build you up, or tear you down, if you allow them to. How could someone who was once so close to God stray so far from Him?

In early January 2002, my military duties as a first sergeant took me to Florida to help with casualty assistance for a close colleague whose son had died in a tragic construction accident. It had been just a few years earlier that I had been with this same man in the Intensive Care Unit when his father took his last breath. The night before leaving Florida to come home, my wife called with some devastating news. She told me that the police had arrested Dad for killing a man. How do you handle this type of news? You expect to deal with someone dying, but not this. This was hard. Throughout the months that followed, we would find out more and more of the story. Dad was hurting emotionally and physically because he had lost his son. He turned to drinking and drugs to try to mask and help alleviate the pain. Unfortunately, during one of his binges he was in a fight that ended in the other man's death. Many lives changed that day.

Month's later, at the sentencing (ironically on the birthday of my brother Tim); Dad admitted that he took a wrong turn because he blamed God for taking his son. He said, "Because of my actions I took the life of someone else's son." Through tears, he apologized to the other family for taking the life of their son. He said that he understood that his words would not bring their son back, but he was truly sorry. Dad spent the rest of his days behind bars for his actions. He, his wife, children, grandchildren, great-grandchildren, siblings, and friends have all lost because of his choices and actions. Did it hurt? Terribly! Do I understand? Yes! Do I condone what he did? In no way, shape, or form! Do I judge him? No! Do I love him? Unconditionally!

In May of 2003, my military duties once again took me to Florida. I decided to take a few extra days to go fishing and hang out with friends. One of those friends was the one I had been with just a year earlier when his son died. He picked me up at the airport and on the ride to his house proceeded to tell me that his daughter was pregnant out of wedlock. I said, "You have to love her through this and be there for her." I also told him that he couldn't be mad at her. She already knew that she had made a mistake and now she was dealing with the consequences. What she needed was her daddy to embrace her and give her security. We had gone through a lot together losing his father and son and then dealing with the grief. We were close and he felt comfortable talking to me about it. I had no idea those words of encouragement I had spoken to him would be echoed back at me a few days later.

On my last day there, I called home as I do each day I'm gone, to talk with my wife and children, to see how things are going and to tell them how much I love them. Our second oldest daughter, who was supposed to be away at college, answered the phone. I was surprised and asked her what she was doing home. Through her tears, she told me that she was pregnant. I told her how much I loved her and that we would get through this. How could I get mad at her? This was my little girl who was hurting.

During times like these, when a child has made an unwise choice, so many parents choose to destroy their relationship with their children. Their child makes a mistake and all the parent can think about is themselves and how embarrassed they are. How devastating to that child. How selfish on the part of the parent. When I got home from the trip, I just held my daughter for the longest time and comforted her. I told her how much I loved her and once again reassured her that I would be there for her.

We moved her back home and she continued her education at a local community college. She was still pursuing her dreams and playing sports. Our little grandson was born in August 2003 and he has been a huge blessing. He is my friend and I am his hero. My daughter is a good mom and we have been there for her each step of the way. She received a sports scholarship and transferred to a university about five hours from us where she graduated with a bachelor's degree in business accounting. She is the first person to graduate from college on my side of the family. It has not been an easy road for her but she did this by perseverance and never losing sight of her dreams. I am so proud of her.

In 2004, our church went through Rick Warren's "Purpose Driven Life" together; even the children in the church were reading the book. Several days into the book, on the day we were challenged with the thought of thinking eternally, our eight-year-old Joy-girl approached my wife and asked if we, as a family, could follow through on all our talk about adopting more children. The Lord had spoken to both my wife and I on the same subject. We figured we were still young and had a lot to offer more children. Our focus was not on temporal thinking; it was on eternal thinking. We began the process of a home study with Children's Home Society, and attending all the foster parenting classes required by the state.

In 2005, we met two sisters, ages six and seven, who had been in the system for four years. They were about to be split up so they could be adopted, unless we could take them on. They had already been through not only the loss of their family, but a failed adoption. Their start on life was not fun for them. We visited these little girls a couple of times and it became harder and harder to let them go and say goodbye. The good news is that we rescued them and have finalized the adoption on them. I am their daddy and so honored to be able to provide them love, security and approval. I cannot see life without them.

Meanwhile, my dad was deteriorating rapidly in prison. I visited often and had some great talks with him. We played games and he shared with me how much he hurt physically and emotionally. In early 2007, the system transferred him to another facility no longer near my home. We kept in contact, but I was able to visit him only one more time before I received a call with the devastating news, in mid-June, that Dad was in the hospital unresponsive and in the Intensive Care Unit. The medical staff said we needed to come if we wanted to see him. They warned us that he was in a coma and non-responsive. I dropped everything and drove several hours to where he was with two of my daughters. Two of my sisters and a brother-in-law rushed to the hospital as well. The hospital staff said we could visit him but could not make noise or touch him.

Here was the strongest man I have ever known at the end of his long painful road. His body was swollen because he had congestive heart failure and renal failure.

He was on dialysis in an attempt to drain fluids from his body. The hospital staff said it would only be twenty-four to forty-eight hours. How was I supposed to deal with not talking to him or hugging him? I just wanted to say "I love you" one more time.

We spent the next few days visiting him often with no changes. We had cried all of our tears. We met with the doctors and they continued to say twenty-four to forty-eight hours. We could no longer communicate with him and realized that we needed to say our good-byes and face the inevitable. We all returned home and I continued to call the hospital three and four times a day to check on his status. Each time they told me there was no change, and they were doing what they could to make him comfortable.

On the night of July 6, I called. I was told Dad had been moved to Hospice Care, and it would be a matter of hours. When I reached the Hospice Ward, the nurse asked me if I wanted her to put the phone to his ear, and I said, "Yes".

Through my uncontrollable tears, I told Dad that I loved him so much and it was hard to let him go. I then told him that I released him into the Heavenly Father's arms and I would see him on the other side. Then something happened that was completely amazing. Dad said clearly, "Son, I love you." I thought I was hearing things. Dad was non-responsive and had not said a word since entering the hospital. I was a mess of emotions when the nurse came back on the line and asked, "Did you hear that?" I hadn't been hearing things. It was so awesome to hear. Dad went home to be with the Heavenly Father on July 7, 2007.

The life experiences I have gone through since December 1994 have taught me much about the impact a father has on his children. This is why I have written this book. I had my father's approval and the last words he spoke to me were, "Son, I love you." I greatly desire to share my experiences and the lessons I have learned so you too may experience healthy relationships in your own family. You have the opportunity to impact genera-

tions in a positive or negative way. The choice is yours. I

hope you continue the journey through the chapters in

this book.

Father Role

—ɯ—

A father carries pictures where his money used to be. ~Author Unknown

The purpose of this chapter is not to take away from the role of the mother. The mother has just as important of a role in the lives of children. The roles of a father and mother should complement each other. It is unfortunate because of the fathers not fulfilling their roles that moms have to jump in and do whatever is necessary to provide security for her children. In order for you to give your approval, you need to understand the impact of your role in your children's lives. Whether for good, or for bad, the words you speak, the actions you take, and the choices you make, will impact your children for their entire life. This chapter will help you recognize some of the mistakes that can hurt those you love and help you deal with them effectively.

I once read a story about a father who took his son out for a walk during the winter. His son walked behind him because the snow was very deep. When the father looked back, he saw that the son was struggling to keep up. What caught the father's attention was that his son was imitating every move he made. He was placing his feet in every one of the father's footprints even though he had to stretch to match his stride. This is a perfect demonstration of the imitation of a child of his father.

Parenting can get so frustrating, and there are not always simple solutions. Raising children is not an easy task. It takes a lot of effort and hard work to raise a child but, in the end, it is totally worth it. Children misbehave and it is normal for you to get frustrated from time to time. If you are unable to handle your frustrations properly, it will have negative effects on raising your children. Screaming, yelling and showing how frustrated you are destroys relationships. I hope that you are like me and you do not want your children to sense your frustration, though at times I know I have let my frustration show. Since I want them to see a loving father, who is there to help them through all the tough times- I work at being a good role model by showing a positive way to handle anger and frustration. We are all human. At one point or another, frustrating circumstances will arise. Your children will learn how to handle them from watching you, not from any eloquent speech you give, but on how you handle yourself. Dealing with frustrations properly will teach your child how to respond to tough situations with their peers, in school, their careers, and in their own family some day. This is essential for good parenting.

Let's look at what some of these frustrations might be. When your child was a baby, it might have been lack of sleep, or they cried too much, or they required too much of your time. When they were toddlers, they got into everything. As they got a little older, they started testing your boundaries and rules. Then they entered pre-teen stages. Puberty comes crashing in, and they seem to turn into an alien. You start wondering where your sweet little child went. During the teenage years, friends really start taking priority over mom and dad. Then there are girlfriends and boyfriends, driver's licenses and cars, jobs and clothes to buy. They ask you for money. During these years, mom and dad do not seem very smart to them. They seem to think their friends are smarter and have the best advice. Do not worry you will get them back, and you will all of a sudden become very smart again, somewhere between twenty-two and twenty-five.

I know there are fathers reading this book that can definitely recall times that they have hurt their child. The question is, when you realized you hurt them, what did you do about it? Did pride get in the way and think, "I am the dad and I can say and do whatever I want to"? Perhaps you did nothing about it, hoping it would go away. I so honor and respect the fathers who learned from their mistakes and went to their children and made it right. For those of you who have not, what are you waiting for? It is sad to see people and relationships destroyed due to the wounding of a father. Restoration in these relationships is possible if you will take these lessons to heart and choose to act on them. A good story to illustrate restoration in a father-son relationship is about the prodigal son.

Luke 15:11-32 gives the parable of the lost son.

[11]Jesus continued: "There was a man who had two sons.

[12]The younger one said to his father, 'Father, give me my share of the estate.' So he divided his property between them.

---

¹³*Not long after that, the younger son got together all he had, set off for a distant country and there squandered his wealth in wild living.*

¹⁴*After he had spent everything, there was a severe famine in that whole country, and he began to be in need.*

¹⁵*So he went and hired himself out to a citizen of that country, who sent him to his fields to feed pigs.*

¹⁶*He longed to fill his stomach with the pods that the pigs were eating, but no one gave him anything.*

¹⁷*When he came to his senses, he said, 'How many of my father's hired men have food to spare, and here I am starving to death!*

¹⁸*I will set out and go back to my father and say to him: Father, I have sinned against heaven and against you.*

¹⁹*I am no longer worthy to be called your son; make me like one of your hired men.'*

²⁰*So he got up and went to his father. But while he was still a long way off, his father saw him and was filled with*

compassion for him; he ran to his son, threw his arms around him and kissed him.

²¹The son said to him, 'Father, I have sinned against heaven and against you. I am no longer worthy to be called your son.'

²²But the father said to his servants, 'Quick! Bring the best robe and put it on him. Put a ring on his finger and sandals on his feet.

²³Bring the fattened calf and kill it. Let's have a feast and celebrate.

²⁴For this son of mine was dead and is alive again; he was lost and is found.' So they began to celebrate.

²⁵Meanwhile, the older son was in the field. When he came near the house, he heard music and dancing.

²⁶So he called one of the servants and asked him what was going on.

²⁷'your brother has come,' he replied, 'and your father has killed the fattened calf because he has him back safe and sound.'

²⁸*The older brother became angry and refused to go in. So his father went out and pleaded with him.*

²⁹*But he answered his father, 'Look! All these years I've been slaving for you and never disobeyed your orders. Yet you never gave me even a young goat so I could celebrate with my friends.*

³⁰*But when this son of yours who has squandered your property with prostitutes comes home, you kill the fattened calf for him!'*

³¹*'my son,' the father said, 'you are always with me, and everything I have is yours.*

³²*But we had to celebrate and be glad, because this brother of yours was dead and is alive again; he was lost and is found.' "*

Speaking of prodigals, we have an over abundance of prodigal fathers in our country today. I want to share some statistics I found on the Internet about single parent homes. Over a third of the children in America grow up in single parent homes, with less than twenty percent of those being single father households. Children from single parent families are more likely to drop out of high school, wind up in prison, or run away from home. Drug abuse, teen pregnancy, and suicide, are more prevalent among children from single parent families. Presently, approximately fifty percent of children experience some sort of stepparent relationship by adulthood, though second marriages have over a sixty percent failure rate, so most lose even this relationship.

How is it possible for a child to gain the needed approval from a father, when there isn't a dad in the picture? Having positive male mentors in your life, though not a total substitute can help to ease the scars of not having your father's approval. If you are reading these statistics and saying to yourself, "I do not fit this category," then think about this: even though my children have me as a father, am I actually there for them, or am I an absentee father by not making time for my wife and children. Is my life about me?

From my life experiences, the role of a father is crucial. I made mention of its importance when I told the story about my friend taking his life and his family's security being shattered. I have also alluded to it many times throughout this book. It is a vital lesson, and should awaken fathers to the important role they have in their family's security. For many this could be a painful chapter if they have had a lack of security because of their bad experiences brought on by their father. I encourage you to continue the journey so that you will become an awesome father for your children.

What is security? It is the state of being or feeling secure. It is freedom from fear, anxiety, danger, doubt, etc. It is a state or sense of safety or certainty. It is something that gives tranquility and certainty. It is protection. Insecurity would obviously be the opposite of security. Back in the mid 1980s, I had a chance to help at a mission in Omaha, Nebraska. My heart broke over the amount of fathers and husbands that were homeless. I wondered how many of them had families that did not even know where they were. On the other hand, maybe they were homeless because they lost their family and security was shattered.

Fathers providing security, as well as a father who has not provided security, have influenced many lives. If you look at a father who is involved with his family, you will find security. If you look at a family where there is an absentee father, you will find insecurity. If you look at a father who honors, respects and cherishes his family you will find security. If you look at a father who has been abusive, you will definitely find insecurity in the home. If you look at a faithful father, you will find security in the home. If you look at a father who is a workaholic, you will find decreased levels of security. Just with these few examples, you will see the impact that a father makes in this area of security.

Are you helping or hindering your children from the sidelines? What type of dad are you? Are you just a bystander (absentee dad) or are you the encourager, mentor, and teacher? Let me explain this in the next couple of paragraphs.

One of my daughters played competitive fast pitch softball. I spent a lot of time at numerous practices, games, and tournaments over the years. I played catch more times than I can count, and when she got a little older she gave me many bruises. I had my share of sunburns, sore backsides and a thin wallet supporting her with her dream. I enjoyed watching her play. When asked who taught her to hit so well, she tells people that her father taught her. She says that sometimes she would get mad when I would encourage her to focus more, when she was not hitting well. Nevertheless, one thing she knew was that her daddy was always there to support and encourage her.

Another favorite pastime in our family is camping. We enjoy camping alone as a family as well as with groups of other families. On numerous occasions, I have observed fathers simply watching their children from the sidelines instead of supporting and encouraging them. I have watched little boys fishing by themselves or with their little friends. Their dads brought their fishing gear but they're back at camp relaxing because they are too tired. However, when one of their buddies asks them to go fishing they cannot wait to get out on the lake or stream. Then there are the kids down swimming and I just find mom watching them while dad is out fishing with his friends. The justification is, again, that they need a vacation. Then it is time for S'mores (the traditional campfire treat consisting of a roasted marshmallow on a layer of chocolate sandwiched between two pieces of graham cracker) and dad is too tired and says they will do it tomorrow night. Yes, it is messy, but it is a great memory for the kids. I would say these above scenarios show the aspect of a dad that is not involved in the lives of his children. I have also witnessed many other fathers who are very involved in their families while camping. The main purpose of this scenario was to get the attention of the fathers who have chosen to be on the sidelines and not be involved with their families. Are you making good or bad memories for your children?

Then there is your role of having a child-like faith. Why is it important for a father to have child-like faith? When I shared the story about the three-year-old boy who fell three stories to the cement below, I mentioned, "With a child-like faith, I asked God to show me that this little boy was going to be okay." Why was it a child-like faith? I felt helpless looking at this little boy's lifeless body hooked to so many wires and monitors. I could not do anything *but* call on my Heavenly Daddy. When faced with a sick child, or a child that has been hurt or a helpless situation, whom do you call on? It does not make a difference how strong you are, or your financial status. You do whatever it takes to make them feel better, and I bet many of you, like me, have cried out for God to take away the sickness. This is child-like faith.

Young children think their daddy can do anything. Take this story I heard one time. On the way home from a family camping trip, a young girl and her daddy were the only ones still awake in the car. As the little girl looked at the full moon through the car window, she asked, "Daddy, do you think I can touch the moon if I stand on my tiptoes?" "No, I don't think so," he smiled. "Can you reach it?" "No, I don't think I can either." She was quiet for a moment and then she said, "Daddy, maybe if you hold me up on your shoulders I can reach the moon." Little children do not have a challenge believing their daddy's can do anything. Are you like this young girl thinking her daddy can do anything? Who do you believe has the power to do anything? A person with child-like faith believes that God has the power to do anything. Even restore relationships. A person with child-like faith admits their weaknesses and asks for help. A person with child-like faith watches as God does the impossible.

Another key time for child-like faith is when our children are going through a hard time as teenagers or young adults. Do you think they just need to learn their lesson, or is your heart breaking for them? Are you wishing that you could do something so the hard times go away, or do you push them away? Do you find yourself crying out when you are alone or staying awake at night because you are thinking of ways to help them? Perhaps you are thinking back to how you were mistreated by your father and had to learn things the hard way. Remember when your mom and dad said, "This is going to hurt me more than it hurts you" when they were about to discipline you? I always thought, "Yeah right, I am the one getting the spanking. How could this hurt you?" Then I grew up and had children of my own, and came to understand this confusing saying.

Have we let our children down? Have we grown weary and tired? Do we have faith that our children will succeed? Do we want more for our children than we had? Can anyone other than God be a perfect father? The definition of perfect is not having any faults or defects. I would say that God is the only one who is a perfect father. Our children do not expect us to be perfect but they do expect us to be a good father and to be there for them. All fathers mess up. That is life; we are all human after all. This does not give us the excuse that we shouldn't even try though! This 'why try' mindset has crippled too many father-son and father-daughter relationships. My hope is that you will strive to be the best father you can and work through your imperfections. Learn from your mistakes, and move to greater relationships with your children.

Being a good father does not mean that you do not have faults. Begin by accepting the fact that you will make mistakes. In fact, the mistakes you make along the way should turn to lessons learned, which should make you an even better father. Some may have to forgive themselves for the mistakes they have made. Children are always looking for heroes. I hope you are one to them.

We Need A Hero!

The greatest gift I ever had came from God; I call him Dad! ~Author Unknown

A child needs both a father and a mother. If both are in the life of the child, they provide important emotional needs such as security, love, nurturing, and approval. Mother's are vital in the life of a child; however, for the purpose of this chapter I want to point out the distinct and clear-cut role of a father as a hero in the life of his children.

How can you be their hero? If you are married, the first step you can take is to love, honor, cherish and respect your wife. Secondly, your children need to know you value them and want to spend time with them. I know when my children were younger they would always say, "Daddy, do you have to go to work? We want to spend the day with you." This tugged my heartstrings out more than once. One of their greatest thrills and memories were the special days I would take one of them to work with me.

Do you go to their sporting events, plays at school, recitals, concerts, take them camping, hiking, or go on special dates with them? You may not enjoy standing in the rain, or watching ballet, but these times will mean everything to them. I challenge you to ask your children what their greatest memories are growing up. You might be surprised. If your children are too young to answer that question, try to recall some good memories from your father, or a mentor in your life. What are the good things your childhood memories hold?

Were you prepared to become a daddy when your first child was born? What were your qualifications to become a father? Did you have thousands of dollars in the bank to prepare you for years of expenses to raise a child? Did you have to know how to drive a car or run a business? Did you have the know how to change a diaper or take their temperature? Did you have the know how to teach a child how to ride a bike or drive a car? Most of these things you learned as you walked through life as a parent.

Were you qualified to be a daddy? You probably didn't feel like it, but loving your child makes you qualified! Some fathers have a hard time communicating love to their children. They just do not feel comfortable because they never experienced how to love appropriately. They are searching for ideas on how to connect with their children. Far too many fathers out there focus on the unimportant things in their children's lives.

Young children think that their daddy can do anything. Take for instance the little boy who says, "My daddy is stronger than your daddy." Or the little girl who says, "Daddy is the strongest and he can open that pickle jar." We all know that fathers cannot leap tall buildings in a single bound, nor are they stronger than a locomotive, but they should be the hero to their children.

What is the definition of a hero? To me it is someone you admire and look up to, someone who is self-sacrificing, and someone that shows great courage in the face of adversity or urgency to help others. If your school-aged child were required to write about their hero, who would they choose? Would it be a television star, a sports figure, a rock star, a teacher, a firefighter or would it be you? If it is your greatest wish that they write about you "my father, my hero" and they do not, even if this hurts, maybe you need to re-evaluate your role and involvement in their life.

Do they see you as an example? Are you the one who helps people in need? Children need to see you as a caring father. Are you approachable? Make sure your children know that you are available whenever they need you. Trust me, they will see if you make yourself available to others but not them. Some will choose to believe they are not valuable because of this scenario. If they are happy, hurting, frustrated or disappointed can they share these things with you and know you will listen? Another important thing to consider, are you a father who keeps his promises? It is devastating to children if a father does not keep his promises. Broken promises create such a lack of trust between the father and child relationships. Do you attend their sporting events, concerts, and school activities or is this left up to mom because you are too busy? If you do not attend these events, it sends the signal that what your child is involved in is not important to you. Unfortunately, your lack of involvement in this area can allow a child to believe it is okay to get involved with the wrong kind of crowds because dad does not care.

When you attend these events, do not embarrass your children because of your bad sportsmanship or inappropriate manners. Are you a forgiving dad or are you continually reminding your children of their shortcomings and past failures? How do you feel when someone continually puts you down? Be a father that builds up your children and believes in them. If you are the parent on the sidelines who is always yelling and putting down someone, ask yourself, "Why is it so important that I am always right and someone else is always wrong?" Do you see yourself in this scenario? You have made the choice to do this. If this is how you behave, what sort of people will your children become? The saying "children do not always listen to you, but they imitate you" is very true.

My father loved all of his children and we loved him. He was a very hard working man supporting his family. He was so tired when he got home from work. Most days, he'd eat dinner and then fall asleep in his chair watching television. Each of us siblings had our chores and if we did not do them, we reaped the wrath of dad. Was he mean? No, but he did raise us with some strict discipline. On the weekends, we usually worked on fixing cars, repairing the pump in our well, taking care of horses, milking the cow, raising the ducks and geese, washing dishes, burning garbage in the barrel out back, or folding clothes. The household chores were no small task as I had three older siblings and five younger ones. Can you imagine the amount of dishes we had to wash without a dishwasher? I can still see the endless piles of dishes and the mounds of clothes on the couch. Mom was busy running the household and raising nine children. Unfortunately, between making a living outside the home and repairing things at home dad was exhausted.

For me, my dad didn't meet the need I had for a hero, though I so desperately wanted him to. I, like many who are reading this, have found mentors and heroes throughout my life from outside sources. I was fortunate enough to find safe men, who instilled good values in me. These men gave me encouragement, guidance, and a strong desire to succeed. Here are some examples of those heroes.

Throughout grade school and junior high, I played baseball and was a very good player, but I do not remember dad attending any of my games. My coach provided me rides and always made me feel special. How about you? Did you find a coach who helped mentor you? I was also in Cub Scouts, Webelos, and Boy Scouts, but dad was never involved. He never went on hikes, never went on scout camping trips, and never helped me with any of the merit badges. Fortunately, my scout leader, Don Honey, took me under his wing and became a mentor to me. He provided many things for me throughout these years- rides, sleeping bags, tents, food, and most importantly, guidance and encouragement. Did you have a man who encouraged you when you were younger?

In high school, I was in the Marine Corps JROTC (Junior Reserve Officer Training Corps) and eventually earned the promotion as the commander of the unit. One of the instructors, Top Daly, became one of my favorite mentors and heroes. He had been a prisoner of war and knew about hard times. He was a tough man, but he was always encouraging and gave me great guidance. He is one of the men who really taught me to be a leader. Did you have a special teacher who mentored you and made you realize your potential?

After high school, I entered the United States Air Force and spent almost twenty-five years travelling around the world. Throughout my career, I found a few mentors. My main military mentor was Brigadier General William B. Webb, who took me under his wing. I had the honor of serving with him overseas at Supreme Headquarters Allied Powers Europe (SHAPE), Belgium. As a young Sergeant in the Air Force, he made me feel important and valuable as a Non-Commissioned Officer.

While stationed back stateside, we lost touch. Fifteen years later, I had the awesome opportunity to reconnect with him. I saw an ad that he would be visiting our base as a guest speaker. I found out his contact information and gave him a call. He was thrilled to reconnect and asked me if I would like to go to the meeting with him. I agreed and he offered to give me a ride. He picked me up in a nice black Mercedes, drove me to the Officers Club, and arranged for me to sit with him at the head table. When he got up to speak, he spent what felt like ten minutes telling the audience that I had made a big impact on him as a great Non-Commissioned Officer...wow. I went on to reach the highest enlisted grade of Chief Master Sergeant (E-9) because of mentors like this who believed in me. When I retired in 2004, I received a very special gift from him and his wife. I still keep in contact with him via email to this day. How about you? Did you have someone professionally who made you feel special and mentored you?

While stationed in Florida, in the late 1990's, once again a man took me under his wings. His name was Jerry Forehand. He is an awesome man who has helped me through so much. We went on some of the greatest fishing adventures, he comforted me when my brother passed away, he taught me how to build houses, he comforted me when my father was going through his tough times, and he taught me how to lead other men. Even though he is many miles from me, he is still an important influence in my life and I am in still in communication with him. How about you? Do you have a friend who you know you can call at anytime and they would be there for you? Are they someone who can speak into your life?

My greatest mentor and most definitely my hero is a man who joined the Army Air Corps at a young age during WWII. While flying a mission over Austria, his aircraft was shot down and he was taken captive. As a prisoner, he marched five-hundred miles over a seventy day period in the harshest of winter conditions. He lost many friends and colleagues during that march. His faith in God and the love he had for his wife and family is what kept him alive as a prisoner of war. When he returned home, his wife, thinking he was dead, had become involved in another relationship. She gave him the devastating news she didn't want him back and wanted a divorce. This news ripped his heart out. After a time of mourning and depression, he pulled himself together, went to college and became a business owner and a veterinarian, married his current, beautiful wife of 60 plus years, and had a successful career. Once he retired as a veterinarian, he became a pastor and a mentor to many people.

This man knew so much suffering and persevered through arduous trials. He also knew great success and touched many lives because he overcame those hardships and made something of his life. In 1989, this man took me under his wings and became one of the greatest influences on my life. I still visit him and his wife, as well as call him for his advice on my decisions. If you want to know more about him, his name is Dr. Robert Otto and he has just written a book, "A Walk with God" which is available on Amazon.com. A part of his story is in the book, "The Last Escape: The Untold Story of Allied Prisoners of War in Germany 1944-45". How about you? Do you have someone who when you are around them makes you feel you can do anything because that person's life tells you that you can?

Perhaps my story sounds like I'm telling your story. Just like me, you dreamed your dad would be there for you. You desired for your dad to tell you he thought you were doing a good job in school instead of criticizing you for low grades. You wanted him to be there when you received your awards, or made the great plays in sports. You saw other dads congratulating their son or daughter, and you wanted your dad to cheer you on and encourage you. You wanted him there to comfort you in your hard times.

I found mentors and heroes throughout my life that fulfilled but sometimes also suppressed what I was longing for from my own father. Some people have fathers that are their hero and mentor. They are the envy of many people. They had fathers who spent time with them and encouraged them. They had a dad who gave approval. They always appeared to be doing something like fishing together, going to the movies together, going out to dinner together, going on trips together, etc. If you are one of the people that have had this kind of relationship I so honor you and your father. My greatest desire in this is that you are passing this type of relationship on to your children and the generations that follow. In addition, I would highly encourage you to become a hero and mentor to other young people who do not have a hero and mentor in their life. The impact and legacy you will leave is immeasurable. Now would be a good time to take the opportunity to tell your dad (or your mentor) how much he has meant to you.

For many people their dad was just a man who gave them life. Many have had to deal with abusive fathers and do not want anything to do with them. Some were glad when their father died. I strongly encourage you to read the "The Letter" in the chapter entitled "Dealing with Offences" and go through the process of healing so that you will not make the same mistakes your father did. It is your choice not someone else's. Make the choice now that you will be different. This book will help you to do this without bitterness, so you do not become the thing you are avoiding!

I understand the hurt of not having a daddy hero. Fortunately, I also understand the good times because of the words he spoke to me at age thirty-three, "Son, I'm proud of you," and the subsequent choices I made to mend our relationship. Once again, I will reiterate that my dad loved me, and I loved my dad, even during the years before age thirty-three. However, I so longed for him to be somebody I looked up to and wanted to be like. Before then, I didn't want to be like my dad. I said things like, "I will do things differently," and, "I won't do that to my kids." I didn't realize that until I received these words of praise from my dad, I was myself doing the same things he had done. I worked hard, came home tired, ate dinner, and then fell asleep in my recliner. Even though I was a good father, in 1995 during this healing process, I focused myself to become the best father and husband I could be.

From that point in 1995, I made a more focused effort to go to my children's events, I encouraged them, I expressed my love to them, I gave them my approval, and I became their hero. Because I chose to make changes in my life, I have reaped a lifetime of happiness from giving to my children, and I know this blessing will continue in my grandchildren. Following are a few of the notes I've received from them. I'm only sharing them with you to show you the impact you can make.

Before I share the notes, I want to tell you about my eldest daughter. One of the best things she does is write notes of encouragement, these love notes are some of my greatest treasures. Just a couple of months ago she signed a record deal with a label in Nashville, Tennessee. She is a talented singer and songwriter. She is also our adventurous and giving one. She loves to travel, and has a heart for missionary work and helping others. She has lived and explored around the world, including Switzerland, Africa, Israel, Egypt, France, and Hawaii. She is currently planning a trip to London. She loves jumping out of perfectly good airplanes and doing things that I would never even consider. She lives several hours from us, so, I do not get to see her often. However, we do speak frequently, and I thoroughly enjoy our conversations, and living adventures through her. I am so proud of her and the woman she has become. She continues to write love notes to my wife and I that encourage and inspire us. Here are a few of her notes to me, as well as some from our other daughters at various stages of life.

"Hi Dad – Words can't truly express what you mean to me. How much I am blessed to have you as my daddy and my friend. You have been my biggest fan ever since I can remember. And you love my mother like no one else! Thank you for teaching me about Jesus at such a young age. It truly made an impression on me, and I am so incredibly thankful for that. How many kids grow up in a home where their parents don't love God? Don't know what true love is? He is my Abba, my friend, my comfort, the lover of my soul. You have been such an example to me and have helped me set my standards high for the kind of man I long to marry one day. You truly are the wind beneath my wings. I love you!"

"Dad – I don't tell you enough how much I love and respect you. You truly are an amazing man! You blow so many other guys out of the water! You have integrity, honesty, and strength. You have a great ability to lead a group. You stand on your morals and convictions. Your relationship with Jesus is real. Thank you for your example and your

support in my life. I consider myself to be one of the most blessed women because I have you and Mom. No girl could ask for a better Daddy! Loving you forever..."

"Hi Dad – Congratulations! I am extremely proud of what you have done. Thank you so much for everything you have done for me. I would not be who I am or where I am today if it was not for you. Thank you so much for everything you have taught me. My relationship with God, and who I am, would not be where it is without you. I love you so much!"

"Daddy – I think my daddy is cool and nice. And he is a gentleman. And very nice. And he loves us very much. ANND he is a Chief and has a lot of people come to his office. And I love him and I will love him forever."

"Daddy – You changed my life and brought me into the family. You are the best Dad! You make me feel special. You make me feel loved. You make me laugh. I love you."

Fathers on deathbeds do not wish they made more money in their lifetime. Usually, they wish something like, "I wish I had spent more time with my family." If you truly want to be the hero to your children and you have not been, I strongly encourage you to ask God what are His priorities for life. God's priorities will always make you a better father because He is the greatest Father Hero ever.

I strongly urge you to take the role you play in your children's life seriously. You need to do whatever you can to communicate to them, love them and give them your approval. If for some reason you do not; hopefully, they will find some good heroes and mentors they will need. I strongly urge you to read the next chapter and see how important your role of a hero and mentor is as you speak and interact with your children.

Five Little Words

—ɯ—

Fathers, do not exasperate your children; instead,
bring them up in the training and instruction of the
Lord ~ Ephesians 6:4

C an a father's approval or lack of a father's approval be life altering? The answer is most definitely, yes! Your words, both spoken and unspoken, affect your children. Does dad love me or not? Does dad value me? If not, I must be a failure. Does dad think I am smart? If not, I must be stupid. Everyone places a value on everything that happens in life, whether it is true or not.

There are five little words with the power to change the course of a child's life. Without these words, he or she will go through life searching for approval. They will be forever looking over their shoulder wondering if they measure up. They spend their time and effort earning awards, money to buy fancy cars and homes, while all the time they're really seeking approval. The sad fact is what they really need are words of approval spoken from a father. In some cases, their father is not their hero, or he has been abusive, or is absent from their life. Some people are able to find these words from a mentor in their life. I covered this further in the chapter just before this one, "We Need a Hero".

What are these important words? Why do we need to hear them? The most powerful words I ever heard from my father were, "Son, I'm proud of you." I can still remember the first time I heard these words from my dad. I was thirty-three years old. I remember where I was, the time of day, and every detail of the conversation that took place. These words brought me a freedom I had never known. I don't know why it took my father so long to speak these words to me. I wasn't a rebellious kid; I was the peace-making middle child of nine children. Dad had told me he loved me, but never that he was proud of me.

If you are a father yourself, I would encourage you to speak these powerful words to your children as often as you can. In addition, continue to say words like "Son, I love you so much," "Daughter, I love you so much", "you mean so much to me", "you are so beautiful", "can we spend some time together?", and sincerely looking them in the eyes, and asking, "how are you doing?" Speak these phrases not because you have to, but because you want to. Set the example of how to express true love for your children. They will in turn treat your grandchildren with that same love!

Love is a gift, one that should be freely given. Once you have given a gift, do you have control over it? Do you take it back? No, you give the gift, and the new owners of that gift can now do whatever they want with it. I challenge you to not withhold the gift of your love when your child makes wrong choices. True love is giving, not taking. It becomes hard to say these words when your child makes bad decisions and suffers the consequences of them. The importance of these words of approval can set a child free from so much bondage. If the words are withheld, I can almost guarantee that they will continue to perpetuate their bad decisions, seeking approval from other sources, whether it is from good or bad role models.

Here is a story that will illustrate how impacting these words of approval from a father can be. In 1995, when our landlord's sister was in intensive care for attempting to take her life, the doctor's gave absolutely no hope of her recovery. I knew no one in the family but our landlord. I went to see him at the hospital. While there in the family waiting room, I was able to share with the family about the effect of a father's approval and the importance of his love. With boldness, I told my landlord's father that I felt strongly that he needed to tell his daughter that he loved her, approved of her and needed her. The daughter was in a comatose state. During the early morning hours, the father disappeared from the family waiting room. Where do you think he went? He went to talk to his precious daughter. To everyone's surprise, she started responding within just a couple of hours. That father learned a valuable lesson almost too late.

Think back on your own life. Has anyone spoken these words to you? If so, do you recall the impact they made on you? Think about your life. If you've never heard these words, would it have made a difference if you had heard them spoken over you? One of the side effects of these unspoken words is a wall that comes up between a father and his child. Years of poor communication, misunderstanding, and lack of approval can create a strained relationship that may not survive the tumultuous teen years, or the early twenties -before one realizes how smart one's parents really are. No matter the situation, someone needs to take the risk and start the process of healing. I hope that if you are reading this book and your relationship with your dad or child is broken that you will have the courage to take the first step in the restoration process. Write a letter. Make a phone call. Talk in person. My prayer is this book will help you take that initial step, and walk you through the process of healing that very important relationship.

Daddy's Girl

—ᴍ—

Any man can be a father. It takes someone special

to be a dad. ~Author Unknown

I n a healthy relationship, from the moment she's in his
arms, and he looks into her sweet little face, a father's
heart is forever bonded to his little princess. He walks
on air for weeks after her birth. When she grows up and
moves out, or gets married, he goes through a two-year
grieving process just as if she had died (even if she lives
down the street!). Sometimes things break up that bond,
such as unhealthy expectations, divorce, alcohol, drugs,

other addictions, or a lack of proper training as a father, ruining even a great beginning.

When Joe asked me to write a chapter for this book, I did a little research on the subject; even took a survey among my cross-stitch friends from around the world at "123 Stitch!" I asked the question, "Did your father ever, or never, tell you he was proud of you, and how did that affect your life?" It's by no means a scientific survey, it ran only a few days, and a little over fifty women between the ages of twenty-three and eighty-seven answered. Of those, thirty-seven percent said their father had never told them they were proud of them, and it had had a negative impact on their life; seven percent said they had never heard their father say it, but it didn't make a difference, they knew by his behavior he was proud of them. Another thirty-nine percent said their father had told them they were proud of them, and it affected their lives in a positive way; nine percent said hearing the words did not make a difference (I honestly don't think they know what a blessing they had!). Finally, the other eight percent of the women were from abusive backgrounds and said it didn't matter to them what their father said, but from my own experience, and years of counseling folks, I recognize the denial in those claims.

Here are a few of the comments posted by my friends: "My daddy never told me he was proud of me and I spent a lot of years seeking approval from boys in school, men in the work place, etc. Even currently, on occasion, I catch myself hoping to please our theater director with the costumes I build. My DH *(dear husband)* gushes and lavishes me with plenty of praise and love and respect, I'm not lacking in attention. And I know no one loves me more or is more proud of me than my Heavenly Father! But an absentee father does leave a void."

Another said, "My daddy tells me that he is proud of me frequently. This has been a source of strength and self-confidence for me, knowing that he is always there to support me and root me on." Finally, another woman answered with a mix of the two responses, "I glowed growing up. Daddy's little girl and I knew it. He always made me feel like a princess. He would brag about me, show me off, take me places with just him and me and in a million ways made me feel special. Until my parent's divorce when I was sixteen. I went with my mom. My brother went with my dad. For the rest of his life my dad and I were not close. He would constantly make critical comments and the last time I saw him before he died, he said, 'you went with your mother', so obviously he resented it for thirty years! The loss of his approval was confusing and made me sad. But I understood it was his stubbornness and pettiness and had nothing to do with me." There were many other stories told that were inspiring, or heart breaking. It was a deeply moving thread on that bulletin board!

As for my own story of a father-daughter relationship, I have two. I do not tell my story to bring any attention to myself, but rather show the importance of a healthy father-daughter relationship. My birth father was in the United States Navy, and an alcoholic. He was disappointed his first-born was a girl. On his occasional visits home, he required us kids to be silent, and invisible. He was abusive and impatient with babies and the noise that comes with children. I am a partial lip-reader from having my ears boxed one too many times. There were no women's shelters back then, and we lived several states away from Mom's nearest family. At age four, after moving us back up to Oregon, he divorced us. Mom discarded most of our belongings, packed the rest in a suitcase, and we journeyed up I-5 and the Al-Can Highway to my grandparents place in the Matanuska Valley, Alaska. We lived with them for a few months in a one room log cabin while Mom reconstructed her life.

When I was nearly six, Mom met and married Daddy. He moved us back down to the lower forty-eight, to his hometown of Seattle, and adopted us kids shortly thereafter. I knew he loved me. I always tease Mom that he married her because of me! In fact, on one of their dates, he showed up a little early. I crawled up on his lap and we chatted while Mom finished getting ready. When she appeared, he suggested they just stay in for the evening and spend time with me! I was his little girl. After they were married, I don't recall him telling me he was proud of me for *who* I was as a child, but he always let me know he was proud of whatever accomplishments I made. As a youth, when I entered that alien stage from thirteen to sixteen, and felt like the ugliest, most inept person on the planet, he had a long talk with me, and told me he was proud of *who* I was. This helped some, but I had a hard time believing it at that point due to the unresolved issues from the abuse in my life. As an adult, he has told me on numerous occasions he is proud of the woman I have become, and of my family. These words are truly a blessing to me. I came to understand the love of God from my Dad, and his loving us unconditionally as his own!

When my two oldest daughters were pre-schoolers, I received counseling and began the road to emotional healing. I have been able to go back and receive all the years of positive input Daddy poured into me. I also wrote a letter to my birth-father forgiving him, and was able to meet him a few years later and see the changes that he had made after attending AA (Alcoholics Anonymous) and getting his life straightened out. Though we are no longer in touch, it was a healing time for me to hear him say he loved me and was proud of what I had done with my life.

I don't feel there is a great deal of difference in the importance of a father's approval for men and women, yet, on one hand, there could be. There is a special bond between fathers and daughters, just as there is between mothers and sons. In most cases, a woman will usually marry someone almost exactly like her father, and a man will most likely marry someone similar to his mother. If this is the case, think of your daughter, what are you setting her up to expect from men? If you don't have daughters, think of this, whose daughter will your son marry some day? She will become your daughter, how do you want your son to treat her? He will treat her very much like you treat your own wife, unless he gets some retraining (if it's needed!)

One of the neatest things my husband does for our girls is when they reach womanhood. Prior to menses, I have "the talk" with them. I explain the changes they'll be going through, and answer any questions they may have. I tell them they can ask anything they want to know from either of us, and we will answer it. I let them know within a few months after their period begins, that their Dad will take them on a date, talk to them about being a woman, and show them how a man is *supposed* to behave toward them. On this special date, he then presents them with a ring and makes a vow of purity with them. It is our hope that they will take this seriously and save them-selves the heartache of premarital sex. At the very least, it helps them be aware and conscious of the choices they make when they're around boys and men.

Over the years, I have watched daughters of friends grow confused as their dad's pull back in relationship from them when they begin changing into women. Many men are afraid to hug their little girls who aren't so little, instead of learning to hug and snuggle in safe ways, they just avoid the whole affair. This sends signals to the daughter that she is no longer valuable, that she's ugly, something to be avoided... Already overcome with self-esteem issues at the onset of puberty, this just adds fuel to the fire. A study somewhere said, a woman needs at least six healthy hugs a day to feel good about herself. A teen fresh in puberty is no different, they will find the touches they need, whether healthy or not, if they don't get them at home! If you're not comfortable giving your daughter a full hug, instead of no hugs at all, give your girl a sideways or A-frame hug. Try having her snuggle on the couch next to you, or learn to sit just on your knees rather than your lap. It is so important for her to know you still love her, and to maintain that safe physical contact. She will appreciate that you are teaching her proper safe boundaries with men!

We were married nearly twenty-nine years ago; since then, I have watched Joe walk through the steps he explains in the chapters of this book. I have seen them applied in dozens of other people's lives, and seen the miraculous results of freedom in their relationships. Please take his words of wisdom to heart, and seek a healthy relationship with your father or your children today! The next chapter "Unintentional Hurts" will deal with things fathers may do that might not be intentional but have great impact. The insights will be eye opening for you, read on!

Unintentional Hurts

—⟋⟍—

How do you tell the difference between intentional and unintentional hurts? I believe that our experience with hurts depends on whether we think someone caused the hurt intentionally or unintentionally. If you believe you are getting hurt on purpose, rather than accidentally, it is definitely more painful and harder to deal with. Repetitive intentional hurts have a fresh sting every time that person hurts you. However, it can be less impacting and easier to deal with if you know the person delivered the pain unintentionally. I believe it is safe to say that if two hurtful events happened (one intentional and one unintentional), the one delivered with the intention to hurt actually is felt more deeply. Some might ask, "If this person loves me, why do they hurt me?" Whether intentionally or unintentionally it will still be important for you to deal with any judgments you have made towards the person who hurt you. I personally found the burden of carrying judgments too heavy to carry. I strongly encourage you to read the chapter on "Dealing with Offenses". The point of this chapter is to allow you to see a different perspective about possible unintentional hurts.

Did my friend intend to hurt his family when he was so depressed that he took his own life? Though it was not his intention, it is exactly what he did do. He thought his family would be better off without him. He was so wrong.

Had my father intended to hurt his family because he was hurting from losing his son? No, but that is exactly what he did.

Many fathers work long hours supporting their families and come home tired. Unfortunately, some of their actions tell the children that they are not important enough and dad does not have time for them. What are his actions? He has only enough energy to eat dinner, sit down in his easy chair and fall asleep while the television is on. He is too tired to attend his child's baseball game or school play, but has time to play golf on a Saturday morning with his friends. This same father still buys gifts for his children, but usually does this because he feels guilty for not spending time with them. I know I am meddling, but he probably does the same thing to his wife. Does this dad intend to hurt his children? I would say no. However, he needs to make some changes to spend more quality time with his family.

What about the father who loves sports and watches games on the television constantly? He tells the children to be quiet, or to go outside and play. He could even give them more chores to do to occupy them. He works hard all week and this is his time. Is he hurting his children intentionally? This is a little bit sticky, but I would venture to say this is not his intent. He just loves sports; unfortunately, he isn't thinking about his children's needs and is sending them the wrong signals. They think the sports are more important to daddy than they are.

Then there is the father who loves to play sports. He might even play on more than one team. After the games, he sits around and chats with his friends or even heads to the local hangout to have a few drinks with his friends. He gets home and the children are already in bed. He justifies it as his time. However, the signal it sends to his children is dad's friends and his sports are more important than they are. Is this his intention? Unless he is a total moron, I doubt it.

Could an unintentional hurt be a broken promise? Let us look at this for a moment. A good example of this is in the movie "Hook", when Peter kept promising to be at his son's baseball games. He allowed his job to keep him from keeping his promises. Can you get into your child's mind and hear them say, "My heart is broken and I cannot take any more broken promises. I do not believe anything he tells me".

I remember many years ago while we were house-sitting for someone. I had to play in a softball game. I needed to stop by our house to change into my uniform. My oldest daughter was with me, she was always glad to be of help. I asked her to take my change of clothes out to the car while I grabbed my mitt. After the game was over, I looked for my change of clothes. I asked her where my change of clothes was and she told me she put them on the trunk of the car. My wallet was in my jeans pocket. I was more than upset and seriously concerned about my wallet getting into the wrong hands. I said some harsh words to her and asked her why she had not put my clothes in the car. She was crying. We drove back to our house and searched around. We found the clothes, wallet, and all, in a bush not far from our house.

I was relieved about finding the wallet, but upset with myself as I realized I had crushed her little spirit with my anger and my words. If I had taken a step back and looked at the situation, I would have realized that she had done exactly what I had asked of her. I asked her to take my clothes to the car, and being the literal child she was, that is exactly what she did. The car was locked so she put them on the trunk while waiting for me. When I came out of the house, we jumped into the car and headed to the game. I didn't think to check, and she had simply forgotten they were there. I felt convicted and upset at myself for what I had done. I had been more concerned about my wallet than my little girl. She was just being a child. Did I intentionally crush her little spirit? No, hurting her was never my intention, but I was so focused on the wallet being lost, I ended up blaming her. How childish of me, thinking of myself and not my child. I went to her and repented. I told her I was so sorry and asked her to forgive me. I then held her and cried. As I wrote this, I called my daughter and asked her if she remembered this incident, and she said she could not. I believe that if I had not gone to her and repented, said I was sorry and asked her forgiveness, this would have been a bad memory that she would not have forgotten.

Over the years, I have not been a perfect father. However, every time I've realized I've made a mistake, I have always quickly repented, apologized, and asked that child forgiveness for my shortcomings. I highly value my wife and children. Saying "I'm sorry" and meaning it is well worth the struggle of admitting I was wrong and made a mistake.

How about the pain caused when a father passes away after he promised that he would be there for you the rest of your life? Did he intentionally hurt you? Were you mad at him for dying? Then there is the father who cannot work things out with mom so they divorce and now you only see him occasionally instead of everyday. Did he intentionally hurt you? Many children blame themselves for divorce and this is so saddening. It is not the children's fault that mom and dad cannot work things out. It is not the children's fault that mom and dad fight and scream and yell. It is not the children's fault that mom and dad cannot communicate. Then some fathers get re-married and they become preoccupied with their new wife and seem to forget about their children. Once again, did they unintentionally hurt you because they fell in love with someone else and married them? This particular scenario causes many children to pick up an offense and they make judgments against both their father and his new wife. Yes, in many cases, mom and dad should have worked things out. However, if divorce happened- it happened, and you cannot change that. No matter how painful it is.

Do any of these stories hit home with you? I would suggest that many fathers hurt their loved ones more often than they know. The purpose of this chapter is to bring awareness about the unintentional emotional hurt that fathers sometimes inflict on their children. It is important that fathers stop this process. You must stop the cycle of hurting. Examine yourself and check if you are hurting your children and then focus on the healing process described in the next chapters.

Perceptions

—∿∿—

There are three stages of a man's life: He believes in Santa Claus, he doesn't believe in Santa Claus, he is Santa Claus. *~Author Unknown*

What is a perception? It is the mental process of attaining awareness or understanding of what we see. For the purpose of this book, I would say that when you observe something, no matter what age you are, whether it was good or bad, your brain transforms what you see into a perception. The perception is now part of your memory. Everyone perceives things differently because of their personal memory bank of information of what they have observed from their point of view.

Too often people expect others to perceive things exactly the same way as they do. People who choose to ignore other's perceptions are more concerned about being right and do not allow others to be individuals. These people get into arguments, fights and unfortunately destroy individuals and relationships. If you find yourself reading this and realizing this is something you do, I would say you must make a choice to change. I would highly encourage you to follow the steps given in the chapter "Dealing with Offenses" and work toward bringing restoration to some of these broken relationships.

Look at these words from the letter I wrote my father, *"Some of these things I saw through the eyes of a child. They may not be accurate; but getting them in the open (the way they had implanted themselves in my mind) is the only way I can deal with them and find restoration."* Because I was unsure of myself, I had justified it in my mind that they were not accurate. I was later to find out that these words were very important and they were very accurate. Even though somebody might have had a different perspective, or perception of the memory, does not make your memory less valid. I conclude that how you remember, or how you perceive something, is the implant it has made into your memory banks. The specific memory or perception must be dealt with according to how it was implanted.

Thinking back on your life, what are your earliest memories? I personally cannot remember things before the age of four. I vaguely remember things between ages of four and six. As I grew older, my memories started to get clearer and clearer. I believe that many people, like me, have justified that the memories or perceptions were not correct because they were a child. Maybe you have thought that young children do not have the memory of an adult. This is called justification. It is very important that you grasp this concept and do not brush it aside thinking that the memories are incorrect. From my experience, and the experience of others I have talked with, the doubt usually comes with the bad memories and not the good ones.

It is also important to understand that everything looks bigger and scarier when you are a child. This is especially true with the memories of a young child and even into the teenage years. When I look back on some of my memories, many times I think to myself, "Why did I think that was so big or scary?" It was as if as a child I was looking through a magnifying glass. I found out that some of my memories became bigger than they really were because I took so long to deal with them. It does not matter how big or how small the perception or memory is, it is real to you. It is also safe to say, deal with memories according to how they were remembered. It is wrong of someone to tell you that your memory or perception of an event is wrong. I strongly encourage you to deal with the memories and judgments the way they are stored in your memory.

Let me illustrate different memories or perceptions with five children watching the same movie. When my eldest was three, she watched Disney's "Pinocchio" with four of her little friends, aged three through five. A week later, those same children came for another visit. My wife asked them what movie they would like to watch and each gave a different, enthusiastic answer, all at the same time. The five year old said, "The whale movie." A four year old said, "The donkey movie." The other four year old said, "The puppet movie." The three year old boy said, "The movie with the bug!", and our daughter, the only girl in the bunch, wanted to watch, "The movie with the pretty, blue fairy in it." It took my wife a moment to realize they were all talking about the same movie! Each of those children had their own perception of what happened in "Pinocchio." Were any of their perceptions wrong? No, all those things are in that movie, but they each had a different memory or perception of it. Different things had made an impression on each of them.

Quite possibly some memories are buried deep in the back of our memory banks by the trauma that surrounded the memory. The memories become very painful when you think about them. Many people have been in depression and guilt for years because of these memories. From my experience, I believe that once dealt with there will be so much freedom and the memories will stop haunting you. I would suggest that with these painful memories come judgments that you might have made towards the other person or persons. These judgments might look like "I am bitter towards them", "I am angry at them", "I am bitter and resent them", "I am embarrassed by what they have done", "I must not be worthy because they have treated me this way" etc. The truth is these judgments are controlling you and not the other person. The next chapter "Dealing with Offenses" will be your door to experience freedom from these judgments and I highly encourage you to read it with an open mind. The choice is yours.

Dealing with Offenses

—ɯ—

D ealing with offenses is for both the offender and
the offended. Let me explain. My father offended
me but I made judgments and picked up offenses. I found
so much healing and freedom when I was able to ask
my father for forgiveness for the judgments I had made
against him.

Many times, we want the person who offended us to
ask us to forgive them. I believe this is backward thinking.
In some cases, the person who did the offending does not
even know they have offended you. A verse in the Bible,
Mark 11:25 says that I need to forgive so that our Heavenly
Father will forgive me. Even if they do understand what

they are doing, the Lord tells us to release and forgive them. I believe that not forgiving, not removing the judgments, imprisons oneself. Forgiveness on the other hand (removing the judgment) sets us free. We are accountable for our judgments, our words, and our actions, not somebody else.

In some cases, the offender knows exactly what they are doing. In most cases, the person who has been offended, abused or hurt makes a judgment and now owns that judgment. I am angry. I am bitter. I am resentful. This is when it becomes hard to walk down this road of healing, especially dealing with your judgments towards the offender. Even if you are unable to talk to the offender, I would strongly suggest, for your healing, that you rid yourself of the judgments. I say this because these judgments weigh you down and you do not need to carry them. This does not release the offender of the offenses because they are still responsible for their actions.

A child's greatest disappointment may come when he or she discovers that a role model's integrity has been compromised by immorality, lying, stealing, abuse, etc. The depth of such wounds may be everlasting if not dealt with. The child's foundation of right and wrong could be shaken. They will probably feel disappointed and let down. They might even blame themselves for what has happened. They could become resentful, bitter or angry towards the father (or role model). Have you ever heard, or said yourself, "Do as I say, not as I do?" That is like asking water not to flow downhill. A child knows what their dad (or mentor) has done is wrong and if they were to behave in the same manner, they would be in big trouble with their dad. However, no matter what their dad says, if he does it then it must be okay because he's dad! Unfortunately, in most cases, a judgment has been made and has to be dealt with.

For the first time in my life, when I was thirty-three years old, my dad told me, that he was proud of me. Those words changed my life forever. I began to realize I had made many judgments against my dad due to unresolved conflict and feeling responsible for his wrong choices. When I came to this realization, I knew I had to come clean with him. For too long I felt responsible for things he had done and carried things like resentment, bitterness, anger, lack of trust and judgment. This was not a fun path to go down, but it was vital. It is a road I hope all who read this book will strongly consider travelling. The destination is well worth the journey!

Please note that I said, "I carried." These things were weighing me down. Before that revelation, I wanted to hear my dad say he was sorry for those things. The truth is he did not even have a clue I was carrying them. He may have done the acts I witnessed, but he did not cause me to pick up the offenses and own them. I made that choice, even though I was a child for some of them, I still chose to pick them up. Most of us hope the other person will ask us for forgiveness, after all, they are the one who hurt us. This was a hard realization for me but as I was going down this road, I knew I had to face it.

A few months later, I woke up in the middle of the night with a compelling urge to write a letter to my dad, asking his forgiveness for these things. I had been feeling the urge to do so for a couple of days, but had kept ignoring it. I did not know where to begin or, even, what exactly I was carrying. I just knew I couldn't ignore it any longer, I needed to get whatever it was out, so I started writing and the floodgates opened. I spent the next five hours writing that letter. Through every event in which I had chosen to pick up an offense, I relived all the hurt and anguish. I cried. I got angry. I felt abandoned. I felt scared. I processed each event, recognized the offense, then wrote a paragraph and asked Dad to forgive me. I never made it back to bed.

When I had finished, the next hurdle was to get the letter into my dad's hands. Was I afraid? Absolutely! Did I have thoughts that I was making all of this up and should just throw the letter away? Definitely! However, I chose to give it to my dad. I handed it to him when I arrived at church later that same morning. After service, he approached me in the parking lot. Oh no, what did he think? I had to face him. He said to me, "Son, I read your letter." Once again, fear struck me. He said, "There is one thing I disagree with." I asked, "What's that?" He told me what it was and we discussed it. How I had worded it in my letter was confusing to him, but, after discussing it, he said, "okay." He then did something that blew me away. He grabbed me in his arms and said, "I am so sorry." Then he said, "I forgive you, son." We were both crying. Then he asked, "Will you forgive me?" I said, "Yes, Dad."

From that point on, I made a choice that I would not consciously pick up another offense, and if I did, I would deal with it quickly. This was very important for me because of the decisions my dad made in the following years. I did not agree with his choices, but I did not judge him, nor did I pick up an offense. This process allowed me to love him unconditionally and walk with him through some tough roads. I loved my dad unconditionally the rest of his life. Did he become my hero? In many ways, he did. I can look back over my life and see all the great things he had instilled in my life. It is because of him and his influence on my life that I am writing this book, which I believe will touch millions of dads throughout the world.

If this story represents you, I beg you to go down the road of asking forgiveness. If your dad is alive, please take the opportunity to write him a letter or have a frank talk with him. If your dad has passed away, I encourage you to write the letter and go through the emotions. Act as if you are giving it to him and then trust that he would say, "I forgive you." Because of this process, there is no doubt in my mind he would say these words. You can do what you like with the letter. Deal with it in whatever manner works for you, and do not let someone else's procedure dictate what brings you peace. Some will burn it as a sign that they have dealt with it. Some will save it and reread it occasionally. Others will share it with others hoping it will set them free.

Below are portions of my letter, which I am only sharing to give you an example. In no way am I sharing this to tear down my dad. Please continue this road to healing and experience the amazing opportunities in relationships this will bring. This will make you a better son or daughter. This will make you a better husband or wife. This will definitely make you a better dad or mom as well as a grandparent. I hope you will take this on as a tool to help others.

The Letter

Dear Dad,

I am writing this letter to you so I can continue a healing process that started last December. Remember on the day I received my highest military decoration- you told me that you were proud of me. That broke something in me and began a healing process. Of all my awards, including the one received that day, none could compare to the words you said to me after the presentation. "Son, I'm proud of you." I weep even now just thinking about those words. Since then, I no longer live with the constant fear of feeling that I am being watched by a superior waiting to catch me making a mistake and punishing me. I no longer need to prove myself to anyone. I am accepted because of five words- "Son, I'm proud of you."

However, that was just the beginning of the healing process. I was approved, but now there were the areas of embarrassment, disappointment, and lack of trust I now realize need to be dealt with. I wanted to run away and not have to deal with it; God had different plans and you taught me never to run from a problem. I still did not know what to do or how to deal with talking to you about these things until Wednesday night. A father and son spoke about their relationship and dealing with these same issues. The scrip-

ture they started with was Malachi 4:6 "He will turn the hearts of the fathers to their children, and the hearts of the children to their fathers." Then they said, "Every problem we face is a relationship problem." I knew on Wednesday night, the twentieth of December, that I needed to write you a letter to ask your forgiveness for the lack of trust I developed in you, the judgments I had made toward you, and the bitterness I've harbored because of some things I've watched you do. I took ownership of these feelings and I am tired of carrying them.

I am not sure how you will respond to these; however, I'm man enough to write this letter and only responsible to seek your forgiveness. How you deal with this letter is totally up to you. Some of these things I saw through the eyes of a child. They may not be accurate; but getting them in the open (the way they were implanted in my mind) is the only way I can deal with them and find restoration. Here goes...

I remember that I loved baseball as a child and was one of the all-stars with the Clearview Athletics. You never came to any of my games, only Mom. I so longed to see my daddy at the games and became jealous of the other boys whose dad's were there for them. This caused me to lack self-confidence and seeking for your approval. Please forgive me for harboring bitterness!

I understand that your body is in pain; however, I have watched people older than you who are in as much pain if not more become leaders in our church and participate. You do not even look as though you want to be in church and are only doing it to appease Mom and us kids. Dad, I know that you dedicated your lift to Christ- otherwise I probably would not be a Christian today. I am eternally grateful that you chose to give your life to Him. I just want you to step back up to the plate and serve the Lord as strong as you used to. You were a Deacon and a Head Usher! Please forgive me for my judgment!

I guess the biggest fear I have had with you were the challenges you have encountered with suicide. I stopped you once. I was so scared. Here was my dad, the strongest person I knew, thinking about blowing his head off. This affected me more than you can imagine. I have wept so many times for you in this area. I have also thought you were going to leave Mom and the family hoping your challenges of life would go away. Please do not consider either of these options – your father left you and has challenged you with a void and possibly a lack of a father's approval yourself. Please forgive me for not trusting you! I need reassurance from you in this area.

Dad, I cannot carry any more of this pain. I need your forgiveness and for you to become the hero I need in a father. I have challenges to face and I need your strong loving arms of support. Step up to the plate – once again! Above all, serve God so we can spend eternity together!

Your son seeking his daddy hero,

I listed many other things in that letter, but I do not feel I need to share all of them with you. One area I want to touch on is the two sentences where I wrote, "Some of these things were seen through my eyes as a child. They may not be accurate; but, getting them in the open (the way they were implanted in my mind) is the only way I can deal with them and find restoration." I questioned myself for writing this way. I started to justify by writing the second sentence in case I was wrong. What I have found is that they were accurate because they were implanted that way in my mind, and that is how I had to deal with them. Even if you make a childish judgment, it is still there. Therefore, I encourage you to deal with them as how you remember them. This process taught me so much about how it is easy to pick up an offense and hold not only yourself, but also the person the offense is against, in bondage. Choose to heal...rather than wound.

How do you begin this healing process? I like to think of the healing process as a baseball diamond. First base is identifying hurt or judgment. Second base is repentance. Third base is saying I am sorry and home plate is asking forgiveness. Repenting, saying I am sorry, and asking forgiveness are hard steps to take for many people. Things like pride get in the way. Some use the excuse that the other person deserved what they got. For some it is just taking the first step that is hard. Dr. Edwin Louis Cole, another one of my mentors, said, "True love is a desire to benefit others at the expense of self." he goes on to say, "Lust is a desire to benefit self at the expense of others." I would say that a person with a lustful attitude does not worry about the other person's feelings being hurt or even worry about their broken heart. Lust is an attitude of self-indulgence. Therefore, a person with this type of attitude will not go down the road of healing because they do not care about the person they have hurt. If you are reading this, I hope you will really look at being a person with a love attitude. You will do whatever it takes to swallow your pride and conquer your fears to bring healing to the relationship and the person you love.

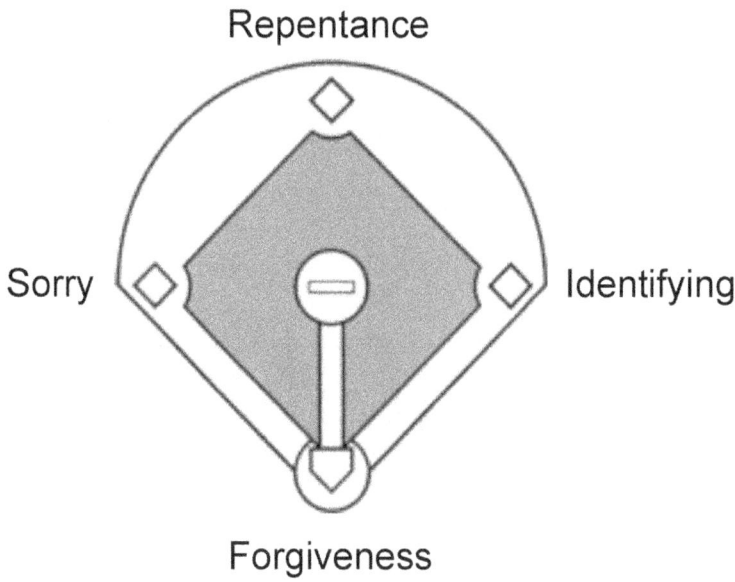

The first step is identifying the hurt. If you need to, ask your child how you have hurt them, then be willing to listen to them, and not try to invalidate what they are saying. Do not try to defend yourself. If you try to defend yourself, you are moving into an attitude of caring about yourself and not them. If you cannot listen to them and try to defend yourself, maybe you are not ready for healing the relationship. This is pure selfishness on your part.

Once you have identified the hurt, and you are willing to continue the healing process the second step is to repent of your actions or words that have hurt them. This is a crucial step in the healing process. If you try to skip this step, the healing process can not happen. Too many people run to first base and then run to third base without going to second base. It doesn't work that way. True repentance is not just crying and hoping someone will forgive you. True repentance is not just saying I am sorry. It is coming to a place where you literally hate what you have done so much that you will change and not do it again. Many people know what they have done, say I am sorry, and never change. They repeatedly make the same mistakes. Because of this, many children do not believe their father really is sorry for what he has done. In order for you to overcome this, you must repent, or else saying you're sorry is just an empty phrase.

After you have repented over the one you have hurt, you need to say I am sorry and ask them to forgive you. If you have hurt somebody many times in the past, the healing process can take some time. Trust has to be rebuilt, and this does not happen overnight. This is why the repentance step is so important because you determine not to hurt them again. The choice is yours. Are you willing to stop the hurting and start the healing?

Accepting and Celebrating Dad

—ɯ—

Children's children are a crown to the aged, and parents are the pride of their children.

~ Proverbs 17:6

Honor your father and your mother, as the Lord your God has commanded you, so that you may live long and that it may go well with you in the land the Lord your God is giving you. ~ Deuteronomy 5:16

The story did not end when Dad and I exchanged forgiveness. Surprisedly, a separation began taking place between Dad and me. This lasted for a couple of months before my wife helped me realize that Dad now needed my approval as his son. I quickly went to him and told him how much I loved, approved of, and needed him. We embraced and a new freedom took root in our relationship.

Why was it necessary to give my dad my approval as his child? I believe the very thing I was searching for from my dad, was also, what he was searching for from me. He wanted to know that I really loved him and that he could still be my dad even though he had let me down. He wanted to be my hero.

As a dad myself, I love to hear my children tell me that I have done things right, even with some of my shortcomings. I want to hear that I do not embarrass them, and that they want to be around me. I want them to come to me for advice. I want them to come to me for security. Even when my daughters are a little older, I still want to be free to hold them, hug them, and give them a kiss on the cheek.

I want to be there for them in the happy times as well as the hardships. Just because they are grown and out of the house doesn't mean I am no longer an important part of their lives. As time goes by, you open the door to being a grandpa. This is one of the most amazing joys in life. There is now a whole new generation you can affect with your love and approval. Some of the greatest phrases you love to hear are, "Grandpa, I love you!", "Grandpa, I want to grow up just like you.", "Grandpa, want to go fishing?" - Or whatever their favorite activity is.

Just as my children want to hear that I love them, and I am proud of them; I want to hear the same things from them. When I started this process with my dad, I was not expecting the other side of the coin. After all, I am the child not the parent. Is not the parent the one who gives approval?

The real answer to the other side of the coin is in the Bible verse that took me down this road in the first place. Malachi 4:6a says *"He will turn the hearts of the fathers to their children, and the hearts of the children to their fathers;"* The first part says, "Turn the hearts of the fathers to the children". The second part says, "Turn the hearts of the children to their father". Turning of the hearts of the fathers to the children is the father giving the love and approval to their children. Turning of the hearts of the children to their fathers, are the children giving their love and acceptance to their father. This simple verse has profound impact!

Losing a father is one of the most deeply life affecting events in a person's life. Just like the disturbance a stone causes when thrown into still water, the ripples of loss continue on and on. These ripples will be either positive or negative; it depends on what we choose to focus on. Grieving over death is a unique experience to go through. The emotions concerned are extremely powerful and most people are not comfortable in dealing with them. Cry and some people think you are overreacting. If you don't cry, people think you don't care. Some people never deal with the loss and sink into deep depression. They don't even want to talk about it. Other people seem unaffected and some don't even really show any emotion. These are just a couple of the coping mechanisms. If you are going through the grieving process, I highly recommend a little book by Granger E. Westberg called "Good Grief!" It simply states the various stages of grief, and helps you to realize you're not crazy, just normal.

Losing a child is something I could never begin to fathom. My brother's death had to be excruciating for my parents to endure. As a parent, we expect to die before our children. Sadly, the ripples of grief over losing Tim were too much for Dad, and he tried to drown his pain with destructive habits and associations. He made some bad choices and these choices eventually lead to his destruction. His choices not only affected him but every member of his family.

When my father was incarcerated, he was placed in the prison in my city. I spent numerous hours with him over the last several years. We talked, we laughed, we cried, we got angry at each other, we played games, we talked about the people he loved and missed. Dad loved each of his children so much, and he wished he had made different choices. During his last couple of years, Dad prepared himself to meet his maker. On July 7, 2007, he finally finished the race. The weeks leading up to this date, Dad knew his life on earth was about to end and he fully understood what II Timothy 4:6-7 says, *"⁶For I am already being poured out like a drink offering, and the time has come for my departure. ⁷I have fought the good fight, I have finished the race, I have kept the faith."* My last words to him were, "I love you, and so do all of your children...I release you to the Heavenly Father and I will see you on the other side." His last words were, "I love you."

I never really realized how much I needed my dad until it was too late. In the last few years of his life, we did spend a lot of time together and were close. My dad had become one of my best friends. It was hard to see him hurting so much emotionally and physically. I cannot help but think back and wonder how much more we could have done together before his incarceration. My life has had a void in it since he died. I believe I will see him again in Heaven when I pass from this earth.

Yes, Dad had his faults...we all do...but I loved him unconditionally and I endeavor to choose to focus on the positive influence he had on my life. He was a good man. I love you so much, Dad, and I miss you. This book is dedicated to you. In a sense, you were my hero!

Father God, I thank you for the life of my dad. Thank you for giving him to us for all of these years. I thank You that he finished strong, loyal to You, and therefore loyal to those he loved. I rejoice now that he is in Your presence. I pray Lord, that even though he is gone, his life will continue to speak positively to those he loved. Father, help me to leave the legacy of a loving life to those who come behind me! AMEN!

If "A Father's Approval" has made a difference in your life, please share it with others, and do feel free to contact me at: AFATHERSHEART@HOTMAIL.COM

Study Questions for YOUR Story

What are some of your life experiences that have shaped your life?

Has your father ever told you he was proud of you? Explain.

Do you believe that the choice is yours to positively or negatively impact your children?

Study Questions for Father Role

What do you feel your greatest role is as a father?

Dealing with frustrations properly will teach your child how to respond to tough situations with their peers, in school, their careers, and in their own family some day. Do you live as though you believe this statement?

Have you ever hurt your child? The real question is, when you realized you hurt them, what did you do about it?

Do you have a prodigal son or daughter? What are you doing to restore this relationship?

What are some things you can do to become a positive role model to support your children more?

Have you focused on your faults and become ineffective as a father? _____. Being a good father does not mean that you do not have faults. Begin by accepting the fact that you will make mistakes. In fact, the mistakes you make along the way should turn to lessons learned, which should make you an even better father. Some may have to forgive themselves for the mistakes they have made. Children are always looking for heroes. I hope you are one to them.

Study Questions for *We Need a Hero!*

Do you believe you have a clear-cut role as a hero in the life of your children? _____.

Are you your children's hero? _____.

Do you go to their sporting events, plays at school, recitals, concerts, take them camping, hiking, or go on special dates with them? _____.

Do you encourage them while you are there, or do you embarrass them by your behavior? _____.

What is your definition of a hero?

Was your dad involved in your life?

Was your dad your hero? If not, who were your heroes and why?

I challenge you to ask your children what their greatest memories are growing up.

Study Questions for Five Little Words

Can a father's approval or lack of a father's approval be life altering? How?

Did you feel your dad valued you?

Has your father ever said "Son/daughter, I'm proud of you"? ____.

Has this impacted your life? How?

How do you believe these five little words can change to course of a child's life?

Why do we need to hear these words from a father?

Study Questions for Daddy's Girl

If you don't have a daughter, think of a niece or other young lady you are a mentor for.

Do you have a special bond with your daughter(s)?

Can your daughter express her feelings with you, without fearing you will judge, condemn, or ridicule her for those feelings?

Do you give your daughter and your wife healthy hugs and safe touches?

What have you done to help your daughter make healthy choices when it comes to relationships with men?

List some things you know your daughter likes to do, then choose one and take your daughter out on a date. Take time on that date to look her in the eye, and speak blessing over her, tell her what she means to you, and how proud you are of her!

Study Questions for Unintentional Hurts

How do you tell the difference between intentional and unintentional hurts?

Can an unintentional hurt be a broken promise? Explain?

Do you agree unintentional hurts need to be dealt with? Why or why not?

What are some things your father might have done that unintentionally hurt you?

What are some things you might have done to your children where you have hurt them unintentionally?

Have you dealt with them? If not, why?

Study Questions for Perceptions

What is your definition of a perception?

Even though somebody might have had a different perspective, or perception of the memory, does this make your memory less valid?

What are some of your earliest memories?

What are some of your greatest memories?

Have you ever honored or thanked the people involved in these memories?

What are some of your worst memories?

Have you dealt with the judgments you made during these times?

Study Questions for Dealing with Offenses

Do you believe that dealing with offenses is for both the offender and the offended? Why?

Have you made judgments towards someone who has offended you? ____. What are those judgments and have you dealt with them?

What are you going to do to rid yourself of the weight of those judgments? (Even if the person has died, you can still write a letter, releasing the judgments!)

If you have compromised your values in any area, have you dealt with this with your children? If not, what are you going to do about it?

Are you willing to stop the hurting and start the healing? What are the four bases in the healing process?

First base-

Second base-

Third base-

Home base-

Study Questions for Accepting and Celebrating Dad

Why was it necessary to give my dad my approval as his child?

Have you given your father, or mentor your approval or appreciation for their positive role in your life?

If your father or mentor were sitting here right now, what would you say to them?

I challenge you to take these words, and then speak them to your father or mentor. If you are unable to do that, then write them in a letter, or on a thank you card.

CPSIA information can be obtained
at www.ICGtesting.com
Printed in the USA
BVHW032335140121
597875BV00001B/18